Reading for Every Child
Fluency

Grade 2

by
Lori De Goede

Published by Instructional Fair
an imprint of
Frank Schaffer Publications®

Instructional Fair

Author: Lori De Goede
Editor: Rebecca Warren
Interior Designer: Lori Kibbey

Frank Schaffer Publications®

Instructional Fair is an imprint of Frank Schaffer Publications.

Send all inquiries to:
Frank Schaffer Publications
3195 Wilson Drive NW
Grand Rapids, Michigan 49534

Reading for Every Child: Fluency—grade 2

ISBN: 0-7424-2822-2

2 3 4 5 6 7 8 9 10 PAT 12 11 10 09 08 07 06

Table of Contents

Reading First

Introduction

The Reading First program is part of the No Child Left Behind Act. This program is based on research by the National Reading Panel that identifies five key areas for early reading instruction—phonemic awareness, phonics, fluency, vocabulary, and comprehension.

Phonemic Awareness

Phonemic awareness focuses on a child's understanding of letter sounds and the ability to manipulate those sounds. Listening is a crucial component, as the emphasis at this level is on sounds that are heard and differentiated in each word the child hears.

Phonics

After students recognize sounds that make up words, they must then connect those sounds to *written* text. An important part of phonics instruction is systematic encounters with letters and letter combinations.

Fluency

Fluent readers are able to recognize words quickly. They are able to read aloud with expression and do not stumble over words. The goal of fluency is to read more smoothly and with *comprehension*.

Vocabulary

In order to understand what they read, students must first have a solid base of vocabulary words. As students increase their vocabulary knowledge, they also increase their comprehension and fluency.

Comprehension

Comprehension is "putting it all together" to understand what has been read. With both fiction and nonfiction texts, students become active readers as they learn to use specific comprehension strategies before, during, and after reading.

Getting the Facts on Fluency

Fluency Basics

Fluency is the ability to read text smoothly and accurately. The reader does not focus on decoding individual words, but on what the text means as a whole. A fluent reader can recognize words, use appropriate phrasing, and read with expression. In order for students to become fluent readers, they need plenty of practice reading aloud. The following are other things you can do to help build fluency:

- Read aloud to your students on a regular basis. (You will be modeling fluency for them as you read.)

- Use poetry that has rhythm and rhyming.

- Do choral reading as a whole group and in small groups.

- Perform readers' theaters.

- Use texts appropriate for each student's level.

- Read the text multiple times.

- Pair up with older reading buddies or peers.

Fluency is a difficult skill to teach and assess. This book offers practical second-grade activities to use with your students and straightforward rubrics to guide you in assessing fluency development.

Key Questions for Determining the Level of Fluency

Does the text seem appropriate for the student?

Does the student recognize most words automatically?

Does the student read in phrases?

Does the student recognize punctuation and adjust reading accordingly?

Does the student read with expression?

Stages of Reading

Movement toward the fluent stage of reading will be a gradual process, and each step along the way is important. The majority of your second graders should be in the early stage of reading, though you may also have students at the emergent and fluent stages.

Pre-Emergent

A student who is just beginning to learn to read is in the pre-emergent stage. A pre-emergent reader will:

- pretend to read
- know most letter sounds
- participate in reading familiar books
- use illustrations to tell stories
- memorize pattern books and familiar books
- rhyme and play with words

Emergent

An emergent reader has gained more skills and is demonstrating a beginning reading ability. An emergent reader will:

- identify self as a reader
- retell main idea of simple stories
- read books with word patterns
- rely on print and illustration
- know most letter sounds

Early

The early reader has made the transition from emergent, but still needs additional skills to become a fluent reader. The early reader will:

- rely on print more than illustrations
- recognize sight words
- use sentence structure clues
- begin to read silently
- read for meaning
- retell the beginning, middle, and end of a story
- exercise phonetic skills
- understand basic punctuation

Fluent

A fluent reader at the elementary level has developed many reading skills and can apply them effectively to text. Some second graders will be at this stage. The fluent reader will:

- read beginning chapter books
- retell plot, characters, and events
- use reading strategies appropriately
- read silently for short periods of time
- make connections between reading, writing, and experiences

Putting It All Together

Vocabulary

In order to become fluent readers, students need an extensive base of vocabulary words to draw from as they read. You will expose them to a large variety of words over the school year. These words can come from stories they are reading, science lessons, social studies activities, and many other learning experiences. Students need repeated exposure to vocabulary words that are used *in context*.

Comprehension

As your students take the final steps toward reading fluency, it is important to make sure they understand what they read. Remember, the goal of fluency is not simply to read faster and faster, but to read *with understanding*. You may find students who become more fluent in their pace and expression as they read, but still struggle to articulate the meaning of what they have read. Follow reading times with questions that focus on the meaning of the text (see pages 51–57).

Assessing Fluency

One of the best and easiest ways to assess students' reading fluency is to listen to each child read. You can take note of word recognition, speed, expression, and comprehension from just one short reading period spent one-on-one with a student. Another way to assess fluency is to use rubrics. Pages 10–15 contain rubrics for both teacher and student use; each one is described below.

NAEP Oral Reading Scale

The NAEP scale (see page 10) allows you to track how students relate fluency to comprehension. Are they reading word by word, spending most of their effort on decoding words? Are they reading fluently, attending to the author's meaning as they go? Assigning a level at the beginning of the year and then again at the end of the year gives you a way to track student progress.

Speedy Word Recognition

Create five rows of six irregular words (words that are difficult to decode phonetically). Each row has the same words, but in a different order (see sample below). Briefly review the words prior to beginning the assessment. The students are timed for one minute as they read the rows of words. Count and record the number of correct words. The students can graph their results to monitor progress (see page 11).

Example:

who	once	of	were	been
of	been	again	been	who
again	who	been	who	of
once	of	were	of	again
were	again	who	once	were
been	were	once	again	been

Progress Profile

Repeated readings of a text are important to develop fluency. For the progress profile rubric (see page 12), the same text is read for one minute each time. Record the date of the reading, the number of words read in one minute, and the number of errors made. The goal is to have the number of words read increase and the number of errors made decrease. Encourage the student to continue working with the text in between timed reading assessments.

Minute Reading

Using the same text, the student reads five times for one minute each time. The partner (peer or older student) helps keep the time with a stopwatch. After one minute has passed, the students count the total number of words read and record it on the chart (see page 13). This gives students a way to track their progress after repeated readings.

Pair and Share Reading

For this activity, students pair with a partner to read their books. The students take turns reading; each student reads a total of three times. On the rubric (see page 14), students will assess their own reading and also their partner's reading.

Fluency Self-Assessment

The self-assessment rubric (see page 15) provides a way for students to reflect on their own fluency skills after they read. By drawing attention to things like sounding out words, stopping at punctuation, and understanding what is read, you help students understand the qualities of fluent reading and monitor their own progress toward that goal.

NAEP Oral Reading Fluency Scale

Level 4	Reads primarily in larger, meaningful phrase groups. Although some regressions, repetitions, and deviations from text may be present, these do not appear to detract from the overall structure of the story. Preservation of the author's syntax is consistent. Some or most of the story is read with expressive interpretation.
Level 3	Reads primarily in three- or four-word phrase groups. Some smaller groupings may be present. However, the majority of phrasing seems appropriate and preserves the syntax of the author. Little or no expressive interpretation is present.
Level 2	Reads primarily in two-word phrases with some three- or four-word groupings. Some word-by-word reading may be present. Word groupings may seem awkward and unrelated to larger context of sentence or passage.
Level 1	Reads primarily word by word. Occasional two-word or three-word phrases may occur, but these are infrequent and/or they do not preserve meaningful syntax.

Source: U.S. Department of Education, National Center for Education Statistics. *Listening to Children Read Aloud*, 15. Washington, D.C.: 1995.

Speedy Word Recognition

Student Name _____

WPM

30

25

20

15

10

5

Date

Words Tested _____

Progress Profile

Student Name _____ Date _____

Name of Passage _____

Date

WPM												Errors
100												20
95												19
90												18
85												17
80												16
75												15
70												14
65												13
60												12
55												11
50												10
45												9
40												8
35												7
30												6
25												5
20												4
15												3
10												2
5												1
	WPM	E	WPM	E	WPM	E	WPM	E	WPM	E	WPM	E

Published by Instructional Fair. Copyright protected.   0-7424-2822-2 *Reading for Every Child: Fluency*

Minute Reading

Student Name_____ Date _____

Name of Passage _____

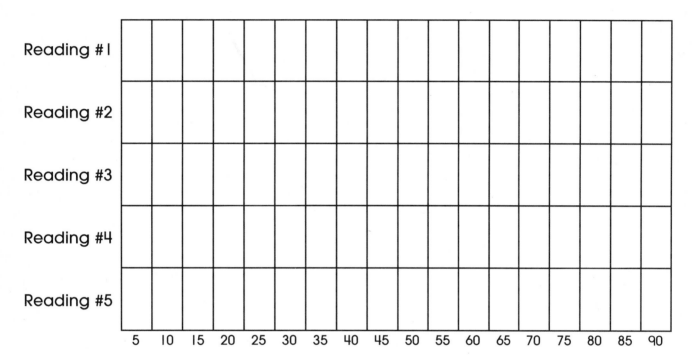

Reading #1
Reading #2
Reading #3
Reading #4
Reading #5

5 10 15 20 25 30 35 40 45 50 55 60 65 70 75 80 85 90

Words per Minute

Pair and Share Reading

Student Name _____ Date_____

Name of Passage _____

How well I read (circle one):

Reading #1:   my best   good   okay   not my best

Reading #2:   my best   good   okay   not my best

Reading #3:   my best   good   okay   not my best

The best thing about my reading today was

_____.

Partner's Name _____ Date_____

Name of Passage _____

Reading #1   Listen to your partner read.

Reading #2   Reading #3   My partner's reading got better
                                   because—

_____   _____   it was smoother.

_____   _____   it had more expression.

_____   _____   my partner knew more words.

_____   _____   my partner stopped
                                   more for punctuation. STOP

Student Name _____ Date _____

Name of Passage _____

Fluency Self-Assessment

Answer the following questions after you read a passage and/or section of a book.

1. I stopped at all periods.

   yes   sometimes   no

2. I made my voice louder or softer.

   yes   sometimes   no

3. I knew most of the words in the passage.

   yes   sometimes   no

4. I had to sound out words in the passage.

   yes   sometimes   no

5. I understood what I read.

   yes   sometimes   no

Using Readers' Theaters

Readers' theaters are a wonderful activity to use for fluency development. To prepare for the performance, students read the text many times. In addition to practice with the written text, students also focus on presentation skills—reading smoothly and expressively, using a clear voice, and following stage directions.

When creating readers' theaters to use in the classroom, it is important to pick stories that will be easy for the students to read (either at their independent or instructional levels). The goal is to have all students feel successful no matter what their reading ability. The more you read the story aloud to the class as a group, the more comfortable they will be saying their lines alone.

Each student eventually takes on the role of a character from the story and speaks their character's lines. (For beginning readers, you can simplify the lines as necessary.) A narrator can fill in the descriptive story action or describe other off-stage events. Long narrations can be divided into two or more narrator roles.

Creating Readers' Theaters for the Classroom

Monday

- Read aloud three new stories to students. (Have scripts prepared ahead of time.)
- Assign students to three different groups.
- Pass out scripts to each student in the group.
- No roles are assigned at this time.
- Encourage students to take an extra script home to practice reading their lines aloud.

Tuesday

- Have students meet in their groups to read through the script several times.
- Highlight one role on one of the scripts, another role on another script, and continue until all scripts in the group have a different role highlighted.
- Read through once. Continue reading, with students switching parts each time until students have read each role at least once.
- Circulate between groups to coach and provide feedback.

Wednesday

- Read and have students switch roles (same as Tuesday).
- In the last five to ten minutes, have students choose their roles. If you wish to keep roles assigned by reading level, you can choose roles ahead of time for students.

Thursday

- Practice reading multiple times for production on Friday.
- Have students make headbands or neck banners that clearly identify their roles (with name and drawing of the character). This makes it easier for the audience to follow along with the action.
- Do a dress rehearsal. Practice reading lines together and decide where each person needs to stand for each scene.

Friday

- Perform!
- Invite other classes, principal, support staff, parents, or neighbors from the community!

Readers' Theater Character Reading Levels

Each character in the readers' theaters will have a corresponding level. This level can be helpful when assigning parts to students with different reading levels.

Level 1—a support character with few lines at a beginning reading level

Level 2—a support character with average amount of lines at a intermediate reading level

Level 3—a support character with average amount of lines, more advanced reading level

Level 4—a main character with many lines, intermediate to advanced reading level

Character Worksheet

My name _____

My character _____

My character feels:

       happy   scared   mad

       excited   silly

My character is:

       nice   mean

My character has _____ lines in the readers' theater.
When I read, I think the lines are:

   easy to read   okay to read   hard to read

Create a headband or neck banner for your character.
Write the character's name in large letters. Add a drawing
to show what your character looks like.

 0-7424-2822-2 *Reading for Every Child: Fluency*

Duck's Day on the Pond

Character	Level
NARRATOR	1
DUCK	4
FROG	3
TROUT	2
BEAVER	2
SNAKE	2

NARRATOR   One sunny day, a duck flew in and landed on a cool pond.

DUCK   What a beautiful day!

FROG   It sure is!

DUCK   *(surprised)* Oh, you scared me! I didn't see you there.

FROG   I come to visit this pond a lot. Sometimes I go up and look around on land, too.

DUCK   Do you live near this pond?

FROG   Yes, I do! I'm an amphibian and have moist skin, so I need to be by the water.

DUCK   Oh, that's interesting! Do you have a family?

FROG   Well, I hatched from an egg in this pond a couple years ago. I pretty much live on my own.

DUCK	I hatched from an egg, too, but my mom took care of me for a while.
FROG	Wow, that sounds nice! (*thinks for a moment, remembering his mom*) Well, I better go. Maybe I'll see you around sometime.
DUCK	Maybe. Good-bye for now!
NARRATOR	The frog jumped away and the duck continued to swim in the pond.
DUCK	Oh, I see something swimming under the water. It keeps tickling my feet. What could it be?
TROUT	Excuse me, you are in my way. I'm trying to find my friends.
DUCK	Who are you?
TROUT	I'm a trout. Who are you?
DUCK	I'm a duck.
TROUT	(*scared*) You aren't going to eat me, are you?
DUCK	(*shocked*) No! Why would you think that?
TROUT	Ducks eat fish and I'm a fish.
DUCK	Oh, don't worry! I wouldn't eat you. I'm not hungry right now, anyway.
TROUT	(*feeling better*) That's good! What are you doing here?

DUCK   I'm just swimming around and—

TROUT   *(interrupting)* Hold on a minute! *(dips back underwater)*

DUCK   What are you doing?

TROUT   *(pops up again)* I had to go back underwater to breathe for a minute. I usually don't come above the surface. I breathe through gills.

DUCK   That's interesting. Well, you better go back underwater so you can breathe. Good luck finding your friends!

NARRATOR   The trout swam away and the duck continued swimming in the pond.

DUCK   *(curious)* What's that over there? I can see wood sticking out of the water. I'm going to see what's going on.

BEAVER   *(upset)* Hey, be careful!

DUCK   Who are you?

BEAVER   I'm a beaver. I'm trying to build my dam.

DUCK   *(kindly)* I promise I'll try to not get in your way. Do you live in this pond?

BEAVER   *(feeling better)* Thank you. Yes, I live here. I love being in the water!

DUCK   Are you a fish?

BEAVER   (laughing) No, silly! I'm a mammal who lives
               in the water. Look at me! I have fur and legs,
               not scales and fins.

DUCK   Did you come from an egg like birds, fish,
               and amphibians do?

BEAVER   No, I was born alive. My mother took good
               care of me.

DUCK   That's interesting. Well, it was nice to meet
               you. I will let you get back to your work.
               Good-bye!

NARRATOR   The beaver went back to making the dam
               and the duck continued to swim in the pond.

DUCK   I think I'm done swimming. I'm going to rest in
               the grass.

SNAKE   (loudly) Hey, watch it!!

DUCK   (looking around) Who said that?

SNAKE   Down here—I did. You
               almost sat on me!

DUCK   Sorry about that.
               What kind of animal
               are you?

SNAKE   I'm a snake.

DUCK   Do you live in the
               water, too?

SNAKE   No. I was born in the water, but I spend most of my time on land.

DUCK   (thinking) Are you like a frog?

SNAKE   No, I'm a reptile. We have dry, scaly skin.

DUCK   I just met a beaver. They do not hatch from eggs. Did you hatch from an egg?

SNAKE   Yes, I did. I thought all animals hatched from eggs! (surprised)

DUCK   Mammals don't, but the rest of us do.

SNAKE   Very interesting! Well, I better go find some food. Good-bye!

DUCK   Good-bye!

NARRATOR   Duck had a very busy day and met many different animals. All the excitement made Duck tired, so Duck took a nice, long nap in the sun.

The First Thanksgiving

Character	Level
NARRATOR 1	4
NARRATOR 2	3
SAMOSET	1
SQUANTO	2
PILGRIM 1	4
PILGRIM 2	3

NARRATOR 1   When we remember the first Thanksgiving, we think of the Pilgrims and Native Americans in 1621 at Plymouth, Massachusetts.

NARRATOR 2   That's the most famous Thanksgiving, but people celebrated other kinds of harvest festivals long before 1621.

NARRATOR 1   The story we will tell today is from the Thanksgiving celebration in 1621 at Plymouth.

NARRATOR 2   Instead of us telling you the story, let's have one of the Pilgrims tell it.

PILGRIM 1   I am a Pilgrim. We came to America from England because we could not worship in the way that we wanted to.

PILGRIM 2   I am also a Pilgrim. Before I start, let me tell you that we didn't call ourselves Pilgrims. That's the name other people gave us.

PILGRIM 1   We came to America to start a new life, but it was not easy!

PILGRIM 2   We had a hard time finding food and growing crops. Many of us got sick.

PILGRIM 1   *(agreeing)* That was hard! We were very hungry and many died from illness.

NARRATOR 1   The Pilgrims were having a hard time surviving in America. They were also afraid of the Native American people.

NARRATOR 2   They called them Indians because Columbus had named them that when he landed in America. Columbus thought he had landed in India, but he was wrong!

NARRATOR 1   One day, a Native American named Samoset talked to the Pilgrims.

SAMOSET   *(welcoming)* Greetings!

PILGRIM 1   We were surprised that he could speak English!

SAMOSET   *(explaining)* I learned to speak English from sea captains who had come to America earlier.

PILGRIM 2   Samoset was nice to us and brought his friend, Squanto.

SQUANTO   I also knew English and wanted to help the Pilgrims. They really needed it!

PILGRIM 1   So Squanto lived with us and taught us many things.

SQUANTO   I showed them how to plant three little fish with their seeds. The fish help the plants grow.

PILGRIM 2   He also taught us how to build good homes and how to hunt.

SQUANTO   The Pilgrims taught us things, too! We got along well, so we formed a treaty.

SAMOSET   The treaty said we would live in peace and help one another.

NARRATOR 2   After all the help, the Pilgrims now had good homes, good crops, and good friends. They wanted to celebrate their good fortune.

NARRATOR 1   So they invited the Native Americans to come to the feast. They were surprised when ninety-one of them showed up! Luckily, the Native Americans had brought five deer to add to the feast.

PILGRIM 1   We had a great time! We ate food and played games.

PILGRIM 2   The celebration lasted for three days!

NARRATOR 2   The Pilgrims and Native Americans had a great Thanksgiving together.

NARRATOR 1   Over 200 years later, President Abraham Lincoln declared the fourth Thursday in November a special day of national thanksgiving.

NARRATOR 2   Then in 1941, Thanksgiving became a national holiday.

PILGRIM 1   So when Thanksgiving rolls around again, remember the Pilgrims and Native Americans.

PILGRIM 2   And the real meaning of Thanksgiving—family, friends, and all the things we have to be thankful for!

THE END

Economics Field Trip

Character	Level
TEACHER	4
KID 1	3
KID 2	3
GROCERY STORE WORKER	2
DENTIST	2
BANKER	1
RESTAURANT WORKER	1

TEACHER	Today we are going to talk about economics.
KID 1	What's economics?
TEACHER	Economics deals with goods and services. We are going to learn about wants and needs, too.
KID 2	I want a new puppy! Is that what you are talking about?
TEACHER	*(nodding)* Yes—that's a great example of a want! Wants are things you would like to have, but don't need to survive.
KID 2	So what are needs?
TEACHER	Needs are the things that are important to survive. Can you think of things you need?

KID 1	I need food and clothes.
KID 2	I need somewhere to live and a family to take care of me.
TEACHER	Those are great examples of needs. You need food to survive, but do you need candy and ice cream?
KID 1	(considering) I guess not.
KID 2	But they sure taste good!
TEACHER	Candy and ice cream are great treats, but your body needs good food to grow and stay healthy.
KID 1	I guess that's why we only get treats every once in a while.
TEACHER	We have been talking about wants and needs for a little while. It's time to talk about goods and services. But let's do more than talk—let's go on a field trip!
KID 2	Yippee! Let's go!
TEACHER	First we will go to the grocery store.
GROCERY STORE WORKER	Welcome to our store! How can I help you?
TEACHER	We are learning about goods and services today. Can you tell us what you provide to the community?
GROCERY STORE WORKER	If you look around the store, you will find many different things people can buy.

KID 1   I see a row with lots of candy and
                       chips!

KID 2   Those are wants, right?

TEACHER   Yes, they are.
                       Great job! Can
                       you find things
                       that are needs?

KID 1   *(looking around)*
                       The fruits and
                       vegetables are
                       needs.

TEACHER   That's right! This
                       store has things
                       to buy. Those are called goods. Goods
                       are things you can hold and touch.

**GROCERY STORE   The cashiers take your money for the
WORKER**   goods you are buying.

TEACHER   Services are actions a person does for
                       someone else. We will visit a place that
                       provides a type of service next. *(turning
                       to the store worker)* Thank you for letting
                       us visit your store! Have a great day! *(to
                       class)* Let's go!

**GROCERY STORE   Thanks for coming in! Have fun on the
WORKER**   rest of your field trip!

KID 1 AND KID 2   *(waving)* Good-bye! Thank you!

(They leave the store and walk to another place.)

TEACHER   Now we are at the dentist's office. Let's go meet the dentist! *(opening a door)*

DENTIST   Hi there! Are you here to get your teeth checked and cleaned?

TEACHER   Not today! We are here learning about goods and services. What do you provide?

DENTIST   I do a service. I check teeth for cavities and make sure people are brushing and flossing every day.

KID 2   My dentist is very nice! He gives me a toothbrush every time I come in!

DENTIST   That's great!

TEACHER   Well, thanks for letting us come in to visit! Have a great day!

DENTIST   No problem! Good luck on the rest of your trip! *(remembers something)* Wait! Take a toothbrush with you!

KID 1 AND KID 2 Wow! Thank you!

TEACHER   I'm getting hungry! Let's go to the bank to get some money before we have lunch.

(They leave the dentist and walk to another place.)

TEACHER   Sometimes I use the cash machine, but today let's go inside the bank. *(opening a door)*

BANKER   How can I help you?

TEACHER   I need to take some money from my savings. I would like thirty dollars, please.

BANKER   I will need your account number.

TEACHER   No problem. *(looks at a card that she takes out of her purse)* It is 124578.

BANKER   Thank you. *(moves papers around, then counts money out)* Ten, twenty, thirty—here is your thirty dollars. Have a nice day!

TEACHER   Thanks. You too! *(puts money in purse)*

KID 1   Teacher, that was a service, wasn't it?

TEACHER   I'm glad you noticed that on your own! Banks hold your money and keep it safe until you are ready to use it. Let's go to lunch!

(They leave the bank and walk to another place.)

TEACHER	This is my favorite place to eat. I know you will love it! *(opening a pretend door)*
RESTAURANT WORKER	Welcome! Are you here for lunch?
TEACHER	Yes, we are. We would like a large pizza and three drinks, please.
KID 2	*(turning to the teacher)* Pizza and drinks are goods. They are food and we can pick them up, so they must be goods.
KID 1	But the worker took our order and will bring us our food, so is that a service?
TEACHER	It sure is! You are finding goods and services everywhere. Great job today!
KID 1 AND KID 2	Thanks!

THE END

Watch Me Grow!

Character	Level
GARDENER	4
SEED	3
SEEDLING	2
PLANT	4
STEM	2
LEAF	2
ROOTS	2
FLOWER	2
SOIL	1
SUN	1

GARDENER Spring is here! It's time to plant the seeds in my garden. I can't wait to have fresh vegetables to eat!

SEED I'm a seed. The gardener will dig a hole, put me in it, and then cover me up.

GARDENER I make sure to water my seeds every day. I have to be careful to not put too much water on the seeds or they will drown.

SEED It is very dark under the soil. I wait and wait. Then I begin to split open and my sprout reaches up above the soil.

GARDENER After a little time, the seeds become seedlings. I have to continue watering my sprouts. I hope little animals don't eat them!

SEEDLING   *(in a small, young voice)* I am a seedling now. I have a little stem that sticks out of the soil.

GARDENER   Now I can see where all my seeds are! I am just waiting to see how big they will grow.

SEEDLING   A little leaf grows from my stem. That will help me make food. I need sunlight and water to keep growing.

GARDENER   The seedling keeps growing bigger and becomes a plant.

PLANT   *(proudly, standing up straight)* Now I am a plant. I have a stem that helps me stand tall.

STEM   That's me! I'm the stem. I hold the plant up. If it wasn't for me, the plant would fall flat on the ground!

PLANT   I also have some leaves.

LEAF   Hi! I'm a leaf. I help make food for the plant. I have green chlorophyll that I use with the sun and water to make food.

PLANT   Down under the soil, I have roots.

ROOTS   *(in a low voice)* I'm the roots. I get water and minerals from the soil for the plant. I also hold the plant in the ground. If it wasn't for me, the plant would blow away in the wind!

PLANT   I also have some flowers.

FLOWER   *(in an excited voice)* Look at me! I'm a
beautiful flower! I make more seeds so new
plants can grow. I smell sweet, so bees come
to get nectar from me. When the bees go to
another flower, they bring my pollen to that
flower. That helps to make more seeds.

PLANT   All my parts help me to live and grow. But,
we need some help. We can't do it all by
ourselves.

SOIL   I'm the soil. I give the plant a place to live.
I also have water and minerals for the plant.

ROOTS   That is where I help! I take the water and
minerals from the soil and bring them into
the plant.

STEM   And I carry the water
and minerals to the
leaves.

LEAF   Then I use the water
and minerals, along
with the sun and
chlorophyll, to make
food for the plant.

SUN   I'm the sun. I keep
the plant warm and
help the leaves make food.

PLANT   It takes work from all of you to help me grow.
Thanks for all of your help!

THE END

Using Pattern Books

Pattern books are great to use with beginning readers. As the reader moves from page to page, only one or two words change. This is an excellent fluency activity because the repetition means there are limited words to decode. The pictures in pattern books should be very supportive in helping students predict the change in words.

Your students can create their own pattern books. Provide a sentence starter and have each student complete a page. Bind all the pages into a book and put it in a basket in the reading area. These are sure to become favorites with your students!

Sentence Starter: In the fall, I like to _____.

Life as a Pioneer Child

Pioneers traveled West to find a new place to live. When they arrived, it was not all fun and games. Pioneer children worked very hard.

1

Pioneer children helped with the crops. They grew corn, pumpkins, beans, and potatoes.

2

Pioneer children helped care for the animals. They fed the horses and milked the cows.

3

0-7424-2822-2 *Reading for Every Child: Fluency*

Pioneer children helped in the house. They cooked and cleaned.

4

Pioneer children worked very hard. They had to help the family start a new life.

5

Incredible Insects

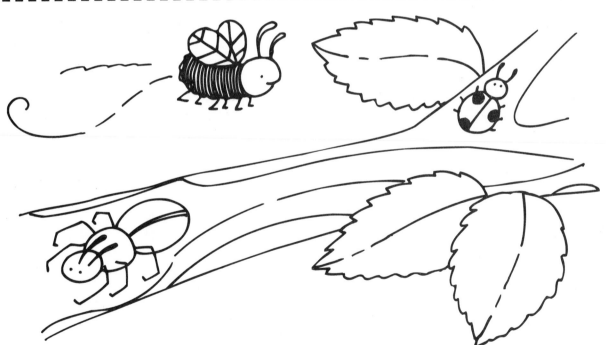

There are little crawling and flying things everywhere. But are they insects? An insect has six legs.

1

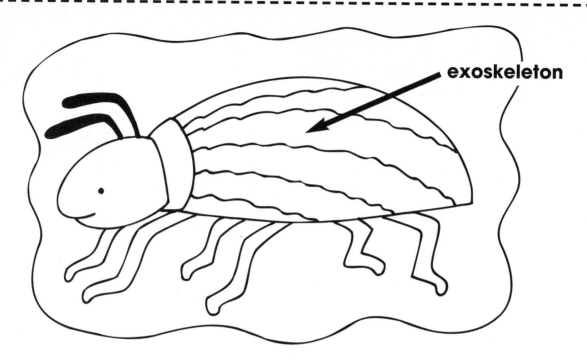

An insect has a hard outer coat that is like armor. It is called the exoskeleton.

2

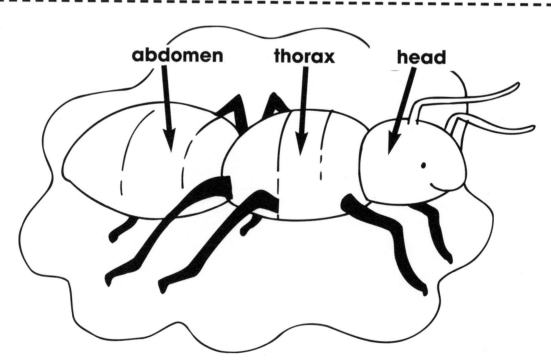

An insect has three body parts. They are the head, the thorax, and the abdomen.

3

An insect has two
large eyes to see
all around.

4

Insects are everywhere! How many different insects can you draw?

5

0-7424-2822-2 *Reading for Every Child: Fluency*

Using Silly Rhyming Books

Silly rhyming books are fun to use as you are studying different phonics patterns. The students really enjoy coming up with make-believe words that rhyme with real words. It is also fun for the students to create pictures to go along with the silly words. This is a great fluency activity because students get practice sounding out unknown words and have the support of another rhyming word to help them decode.

To create your own silly rhyming books, list words from the phonics pattern you are working with. Then make up silly words to rhyme with other words. Put the two words—one real and one silly—into sentences and illustrate. Second graders love this activity as they play with sounds in words!

The scrone made a call on the phone.

1

A twold found a ring made of gold.

2

The zoast had some peanut butter toast.

3

A frole dug a very deep hole.

4

The drow played all day in the snow.

5

"Far, Fur, For"
R-controlled
Vowel Words

The shark jumped from the ocean into my yard.

1

0-7424-2822-2 *Reading for Every Child: Fluency*

The germs got together in a big herd.

2

The yellow bird flew into the scarecrow's shirt.

3

A horse hid from the storm on the front porch.

4

The boy wanted to surf on his way to church.

5

Using Short Reading Passages with Comprehension Questions

Short reading passages with comprehension questions work well with the nonfiction material you teach in other subjects, such as social studies or science. Simplify a nonfiction book or make up a passage of your own. You can include key vocabulary words without having the reading become too lengthy.

It is important to follow the reading passage with comprehension questions to be sure that students understand what they have read. As many readers improve their oral reading, some still struggle with finding meaning in the text. It is important to ask comprehension questions to be sure that students are not just reading smoothly out loud, but also understanding what they have read. No matter how smoothly students read out loud, they are not considered fluent readers until they demonstrate comprehension.

Rocks

Directions: Read the passage below.
Then answer the questions on page 53.

You can find rocks everywhere!
They are not all the same, though.
There are three different kinds of rocks:
sedimentary, igneous, and metamorphic.
Rocks are different because of the way they were formed.

A **sedimentary** rock is made up of
tiny pieces of rock, called
sediment, that are cemented
together. It takes a long time for
sedimentary rocks to form. Water,
wind, waves, and gravity can all
help to make sedimentary rocks.

Igneous rocks are formed when
lava cools and becomes hard.
The lava that flows or shoots from
a volcano slowly cools off and
turns into igneous rock. You can
tell it is an igneous rock by the
shiny crystals.

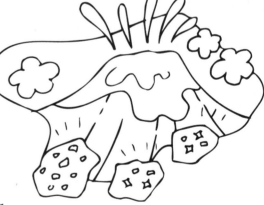

Rocks that have changed are called
metamorphic rocks. A sedimentary or
igneous rock can be changed by pressure
and heat. Metamorphic rocks are new rocks made
from old rocks.

The next time you find a rock, look closely to see if you can
tell what kind it is!

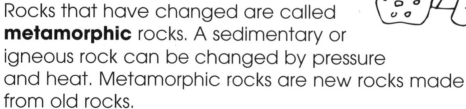

Rocks (cont.)

Directions: Use the passage on page 52 to answer the questions below.

1. All rocks are formed the same way.
   a. true
   b. false

2. Sedimentary rocks take a long time to form.
   a. true
   b. false

3. Sedimentary rocks can be formed by—
   a. wind.
   b. waves.
   c. gravity.
   d. all of the above

4. What kind of rock has crystals?
   a. sedimentary
   b. igneous
   c. metamorphic
   d. none of the above

5. _____ rocks are new rocks made from old rocks.
   a. Sedimentary
   b. Igneous
   c. Metamorphic
   d. all of the above

0-7424-2822-2 *Reading for Every Child: Fluency*

Weather

Directions: Read the passage below.
Then answer the questions on page 55.

Most of the time, the weather is mild.
But every once in a while, there can be
severe weather such as thunderstorms,
hurricanes, tornadoes, and blizzards.

Thunderstorms are very common. They have strong winds,
heavy rain, thunder, and lightning. Thunder and lightning
happen at the same, but you see the lightning first
because light travels faster than sound.

Many people who live by oceans have seen **hurricanes**.
Very strong winds, heavy rain, and waves cause
hurricanes. Hurricanes are given names like Andrew or
Hugo. They can cause floods and a lot of damage.

The most violent storms are **tornadoes**. They
are big funnels of wind that carry things
such as dirt, leaves, and other objects. The
wind in a tornado swirls at 400 mph or
more. Tornadoes cause a lot of damage to
things in their path.

Blizzards are dangerous snowstorms. They
have heavy snow and strong winds.
Sometimes when there is a blizzard,
businesses and schools close, power goes
out, and people get into car accidents.

Severe weather can happen
anywhere, so it is good to be
prepared and know what to do
to stay safe!

Weather (cont.)

Directions: Use the passage on page 54 to answer the questions below.

1. Is light rain or snow severe weather?
   a. yes
   b. no

2. In a thunderstorm, you see lightning before you hear thunder because—
   a. lightning happens first.
   b. you can see better than you can hear.
   c. light travels faster than sound.
   d. none of the above

3. Severe weather with very strong winds and rain is a—
   a. tornado.
   b. thunderstorm.
   c. blizzard.
   d. none of the above

4. A _____ has wind blowing at 400 mph or more.
   a. thunderstorm
   b. blizzard
   c. tornado
   d. none of the above

5. _____ are given names, like those of people.
   a. Hurricanes
   b. Tornadoes
   c. Thunderstorms
   d. Blizzards

0-7424-2822-2 *Reading for Every Child: Fluency*

The Water Cycle

Directions: Read the passage below.
Then answer the questions on page 57.

Where does the rain come from? It comes
down from clouds in the sky, but the clouds
do not make the rain. Rain comes from water that was
already on the Earth. It goes through the water cycle over
and over again.

As the sun shines, it heats up the water. As
the water gets warmer, it changes into water
vapor. This is called **evaporation**.
Evaporation is the reason a puddle dries up
after rain and wet clothes dry on a
clothesline. If you leave out a glass of water,
it will slowly disappear over a few days.

The water vapor rises into the air and groups together to
form clouds. This is called **condensation**. Up in the air, the
water vapor cools back down and forms water droplets.
You can see condensation on the outside of a cold glass
on a warm day. The air is warm and the glass is cool, so the
water vapor in the air turns back to water droplets on the
side of the glass.

The water droplets in the sky form a cloud. As the cloud
becomes heavy, it begins to rain. This is called
precipitation. Precipitation can be rain, snow,
or hail, depending on the temperature. The
falling precipitation lands on Earth and fills
lakes, oceans, rivers, and even puddles.
Then the water cycle begins again.

The Water Cycle (cont.)

Directions: Use the passage on page 56 to answer the questions below.

1. The water cycle never ends.
   a. true
   b. false

2. Water droplets on the outside of a glass on a warm day are caused by—
   a. evaporation.
   b. condensation.
   c. precipitation.
   d. all of the above

3. Water vapor turns to water droplets when—
   a. the sun shines.
   b. they are cooled down.
   c. they are warmed up.
   d. none of the above

4. Precipitation is—
   a. hail.
   b. rain.
   c. snow.
   d. all of the above

5. _____ is when water droplets turn to water vapor.
   a. Evaporation
   b. Condensation
   c. Precipitation
   d. The water cycle

Using Choral Reading
with Two Parts

Choral reading can become mundane after a while. Using choral reading passages with two reading parts spices it up a little! These passages require the students to follow along closely so they can chime in on their part. This also prepares students for readers' theaters.

You can turn any reading into choral reading with two or more parts. It can be as simple as reading every other sentence, every other page, or every other paragraph. How you group students is up to you, but second graders love to be split into boys and girls.

Think about the topics you teach and come up with some choral reading activities of your own!

0-7424-2822-2 *Reading for Every Child: Fluency*

Getting Along and Working Together

Directions: Choose one person to read part A and one to read part B. Then answer the questions on page 61.

A   Our class needs some help!

B   Why? What's the problem?

A   We don't work very well together.

B   Maybe you're right. What can we do?

A   First, we need to have respect for each other and for our teacher.

B   What does that mean?

A   It means to care about other people's feelings and beliefs. It also means being kind to people and respecting their things.

B   Does that mean we follow our teacher's directions and take good care of the things in our classroom?

A   Exactly!

B   That sounds like a great idea! Another good idea is to have responsibility.

A   That's a big word! What is responsibility?

B   It is doing your part so others can count on you.

Getting Along and Working Together (cont.)

A Oh, like when we each have a job in the classroom?

B Yes, that's it!

A Those both sound like great ideas. What about cooperation? That is very important in a classroom!

B Cooperation? What's that?

A Cooperation is working together for a common goal.

B Is working well together in groups cooperation?

A It sure is!

B Some other important things are effort and perseverance. Effort means to always do your best. Perseverance means to keep working when things get difficult.

A Friendship and caring also make a classroom a great place to be! Friendship is making and keeping friends. Caring is to feel concern for others.

B If we do all these things, our classroom will be the best ever!

A Sounds like a plan!

0-7424-2822-2 *Reading for Every Child: Fluency*

Getting Along and Working Together (cont.)

Directions: Use the passage on pages 59–60 to answer the questions below.

1. Friendship is—
   a. working together.
   b. doing your best.
   c. making and keeping friends.

2. What was the problem in this class?

   _____

   _____

3. Working together for a common goal is—
   a. effort.
   b. cooperation.
   c. respect.

4. Responsibility is doing your part to make the classroom a great place to be and learn.
   a. true
   b. false

5. What can you do to help make your classroom a great place to be and learn?

   _____

   _____

December Celebrations Around the World

Directions: Choose one person to read part A and one to read part B. Then answer the questions on page 64.

A   December is full of fun holidays all over the world!

B   Are you talking about Christmas?

A   Christmas is one holiday in December, but many people celebrate other holidays.

B   Like what?

A   Well, in Germany, children celebrate St. Nicholas Day on December 6.

B   Yes, I know that one. They leave their boots on the front step for St. Nicholas to leave gifts and treats.

A   Kids in the Netherlands also celebrate on December 6, but they leave out their wooden shoes. They call St. Nicholas **Sinterklaas**.

B   That sounds like fun! My friend Anna celebrates Saint Lucia Day on December 13. Her grandmother's family is from Sweden.

A   I haven't heard of that holiday. How do they celebrate?

B   The oldest girl in the family dresses like Saint Lucia and serves buns and coffee to her family in bed.

December Celebrations Around the World (cont.)

A   That sounds like a nice way to start the day! Other December celebrations last a long time. On December 16, people in Mexico begin celebrating Las Posadas. These are special Christmas parties for nine nights.

B   A party nine nights in a row? Wow, that must be great!

A   People who celebrate Hanukkah also have a longer celebration. They light the menorah candles on eight nights and celebrate afterwards with songs and gifts.

B   I just remembered another holiday that is celebrated on more than one day. It is called Kwanzaa.

A   Kwanzaa? What's that?

B   Kwanzaa is a harvest festival celebrated by African-American people from December 26 to January 1. They use a candle holder called a **kinara**.

A   Kids all over the world have fun holidays in December, don't they?

B   They sure do! Holidays are special times for all of us to enjoy with family and friends.

December Celebrations
Around the World (cont.)

Directions: Use the passage on pages 62–63 to answer the questions below.

1. Which holiday is celebrated for eight nights?
   a. Hanukkah
   b. Kwanzaa
   c. Las Posadas

2. Where is Saint Lucia Day celebrated?
   a. Mexico
   b. Sweden
   c. Africa

3. What do children in the Netherlands leave out for St. Nicholas?
   a. tennis shoes
   b. stockings
   c. wooden shoes

4. All children around the world celebrate Christmas.
   a. true
   b. false

5. Which holiday do many African-American people celebrate?
   a. Kwanzaa
   b. St. Nicholas Day
   c. Sinterklaas

Shape Guessing Game

Directions: Choose one person to read part A and one to read part B. Then answer the questions on page 67.

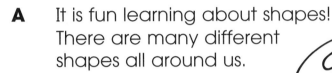

A   It is fun learning about shapes! There are many different shapes all around us.

B   Let's play a shape guessing game!

A   Sounds like fun! You go first.

B   Okay. Let's see. I know one! This shape is round with no flat sides.

A   Is it a circle?

B   Close! It is a 3-D shape and looks like a ball.

A   I got it! It's a sphere. Now you guess. My shape has six sides and is flat.

B   Is it a hexagon?

A   Wow, you got it in one try!

B   Here's another one: This 3-D shape has a flat side in the shape of a circle.

A   Is it a cylinder?

B   Well, a cylinder has two flat sides shaped like a circle. This shape only has one and comes to a point on the other end.

Shape Guessing Game (cont.)

A   I know! It's a cone!

B   Right! Great job!

A   The next shape is a 3-D square.

B   Is it a cube?

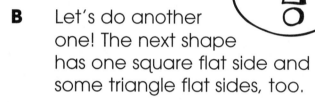

A   Yes, that's it!

B   Let's do another one! The next shape has one square flat side and some triangle flat sides, too.

A   Hmmm, that's a hard one. Can you give another clue?

B   You can see this shape in Egypt.

A   A pyramid! Last one: This shape has four equal sides.

B   Is it a square?

A   Close, but it leans to the side and has no right angles.

B   Oh, a rhombus!

A   Good job!

B   That was fun to play the shape guessing game! Let's do it again sometime!

Shape Guessing Game (cont.)

Directions: Use the passage on pages 65–66 to answer the questions below.

1. What 3-D shape has no flat sides?
   a. cube
   b. cone
   c. sphere

2. This shape is a 3-D square.
   a. pyramid
   b. cylinder
   c. cube

3. A cone has two circle flat sides.
   a. true
   b. false

4. The shape that looks like a square, but leans to the side and has no right angles is a—
   a. pentagon.
   b. rhombus.
   c. hexagon.

5. Which 3-D shape has one square flat side and comes to a point on the other side?
   a. pyramid
   b. sphere
   c. cone

Using Poems

Poetry for Fluency Practice

Poems can enhance your students' reading expression, fluency, and love for reading! You can never read too many poems! Here are some suggestions for how to use poems in the classroom.

- Provide your students with a poem folder to keep copies of the texts you use in the classroom. A folder with fasteners works the best. The students really enjoy reading these in their spare time and it is a fun keepsake from the school year. It is also a great way to encourage repeated readings.

- Put the poems you use most often on poster board and laminate them. It is also helpful to copy them onto an overhead sheet. This makes them easy to read as a whole class.

- Write the lines from classroom poems on sentence strips. You can leave them as whole sentences or cut them into chunks of a couple words each. The students need to put the puzzle back together. These can be stored in a large envelope with a copy of the poem attached to the front for reference.

- Provide your students with a fun family reading experience! Copy poems and send them home with an activity for the family to complete. Another idea is to attach all the poems for the year to heavy paper and laminate. Then rotate the poems so each student takes a different one home each week. This is great reading material to share with parents.

- Highlight a poem that relates to what you are learning as the "poem of the week." It is amazing how many poems you can find that relate to the topics you teach!

- Encourage your students to write their own poetry! Use the poems on pages 70–73 as a guide for some simple poem forms that your second-graders might try. There is no reason that fluency has to be developed using something someone else has written! Students who wish to share can read their own poems aloud to the class.

A Week's Worth of Poetry Activities

Use the following structure for the poems on pages 70–73 or any other poetry work you are using in class.

Monday

Read the poem out loud three times to your students. Ask students several questions about the poem. Have them use highlighters to identify the vocabulary they do not know. Ask students to work in pairs to look up the unknown words. (Some students may claim to, or may actually know all the words in the poem. If they do, ask them to help another student.)

Tuesday

Read the poem aloud to your students. Ask the students several questions about the poem. Have the class read the poem out loud together three times (*choral reading*). Ask students to illustrate the poem.

Wednesday

Read the poem together as a class several times. Ask individual volunteers to read the poem out loud. Ask volunteers to act out the poem or certain words in the poem.

Thursday

Read the poem together as a class several times. Then, alternate reading with the class—you read one line, the class reads the next line (*echo reading*).

Friday

Read the poem together as a class. Have students alternate reading the poem in pairs. One person reads, and the other sits with a copy of the poem and marks each time the reader paused (vertical slash line), said a word with emphasis (underline), or stumbled over a word (check mark over word).

Acrostic Poem

Directions: Listen to your teacher read the poem below. As your teacher reads, circle any words you do not know. Look up those words. Then read the poem aloud several times.

I n a lake or ocean
S mall or large
L and surrounded by water
A ustralia is an island
N eed a bridge, boat or plane to get there
D oes not touch other land

L and surrounds them
A lmost all are fresh water
K ids like to swim there
E ven adults do, too!

70

Cinquain Poem

Directions: Read the poem aloud with your class. As you read along, try to match the speed and expression of the group. What pictures does the poem create in your mind? What messages does the poem give you? Discuss as a class or in groups.

Trash

Smelly and Ugly

Rotting, Stinking, Polluting

Please Do Not Litter!

Garbage

Five Senses Poem

Directions: Read the poem aloud, using your best expressive voice. Try acting out the poem as you read. Next, create a five senses poem of your own about a different fruit or vegetable. Use the poem below as a model.

Carrots

orange and long

sweet and tasty

smooth and hard

fresh and good

crunching in my mouth

Carrots

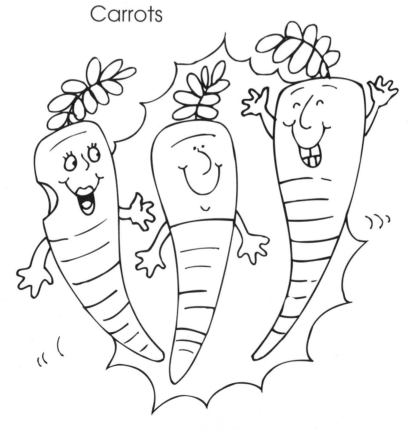

Pyramid Poem

Directions: A pyramid poem describes a person or thing. The first line is the title (one word). Each additional line describes the title and adds one more word. Read the poem below with a partner. Take turns reading every other line (your partner reads the first line, you read the second, and so on).

Maps

have symbols

and show directions

using a compass rose.

There are lots of different maps:

street maps, weather maps, state maps.

They all help us in different ways.

Using Punctuation Activities

Punctuation plays an important part in reading fluency. Improving students' understanding of punctuation is key to helping them read more smoothly. Explain to students that punctuation marks are like little signs that tell us to do something as we read. For example, a period is like a stop sign. When we come to the end of a sentence, we stop before going on to the next sentence. As students are learning to read, they need to have practice adjusting their reading for punctuation.

The activities on pages 75–77 are for students to practice reading sentences using punctuation as a guide to expression. You can also easily create similar activities to go along with stories you are reading or topics you are studying in other content areas.

Periods and Exclamation Points

Directions: Read the paragraph and add a period (**.**) or exclamation point (**!**) after each sentence. When you are finished, practice reading the paragraph with expression. How does the punctuation help you know how to read?

I went to the zoo on Saturday It was really fun We saw

many different animals, but the monkeys are my favorite

The monkeys were climbing all around One almost fell out

of a tree After the zoo, we went to get ice cream It was a

great way to spend the day

Fluency

Question Marks

Directions: Write eight sentences, with a mixture of telling (**declarative**) sentences and some asking (**interrogative**) sentences. DO NOT put the punctuation at the end. Trade papers with a partner and add the correct punctuation— either a period (**.**) or exclamation mark (**!**).

1. _____

_____

2. _____

_____

3. _____

_____

4. _____

_____

5. _____

_____

6. _____

_____

7. _____

_____

8. _____

_____

Quotation Marks

Directions: Read each paragraph and add quotation marks (" ") where someone is speaking. When you are finished, reread each paragraph using a different voice for each character.

Paragraph 1

Hi, Tom! said Jacob.

Hi, said Tom.

Are you going to play in the game this week? asked Jacob.

If I pass my math test I will. My mom and dad said school comes first, said Tom.

Do you need help studying? asked Jacob.

That would be great! I need the help, replied Tom.

Well, we need your help in the game, too! said Jacob. Let's go study.

Paragraph 2

What are you doing? asked Serita.

I'm cleaning my room before Mom gets home, said Deshaun. Why?

I need your help, replied Serita.

With what? asked Deshaun.

I can't find my new markers, said Serita.

Well, help me clean my room and then I will help you look, said Deshaun.

Okay, said Serita. After a few minutes of helping her brother, Serita was surprised. Hey, I found my markers! she shouted.

Oh yeah, I forgot that I borrowed those from you, said Deshaun. I must have lost them in my messy room! Sorry!

Resources

Patterned Literature Books for Reading and Writing

A Dark Dark Tale—by Ruth Brown

Bears—by Ruth Krauss

Brown Bear, Brown Bear, What Do You See?—by Bill Martin Jr.

Camel Who Took a Walk—by Jack Tworkov

The Doorbell Rang—by Pat Hutchins

Fortunately—by Remy Charlip

Goodnight Moon—by Margaret Wise Brown

Goodnight, Mr. Beetle—by Leland Jacobs

If I Had a Tail—by Karen Clemens Warrick

Jesse Bear, What Will You Wear?—by Nancy Carlstrom

Jump, Frog, Jump—by Robert Kalan

One Monday Morning—by Uri Shulevitz

Rain Makes Applesauce—by Julian Scheer

Squawk to the Moon, Little Goose—by Edna Preston

The Very Busy Spider—by Eric Carle

Wheels on the Bus—by Mary Ann Kovalski

Who Sank the Boat?—by Pamela Allen

Why Mosquitoes Buzz in People's Ears—by Verna Aardema

Poetry Collections

A Giraffe and a Half—by Shel Silverstein

A Pizza the Size of the Sun—by Jack Prelutsky

A Poem a Day—by Helen H. Moore

Poems to Count On—by Sandra Liatsos

Poems to Grow On: Poetry Activities for Young Children—by Mabel Chandler Duch

The Super Book of Phonics Poems—by Linda B. Ross

Good Books for
Second-Grade Reading Teachers

"Best Practice"? Insights on Literacy Instruction from an Elementary Classroom—by Margaret Taylor Stewart

Beyond Storybooks: Young Children and the Shared Book Experience—by Judith Pollard Slaughter

Book Talk and Beyond: Children and Teachers Respond to Literature—editors: Nancy L. Roser, Miriam G. Martinez

Celebrating Children's Choices: 25 Years of Children's Favorite Books—by Arden DeVries Post, Marilyn Scott, Michelle Theberge

Developing Reading-Writing Connections: Strategies from the Reading Teacher—editors: Timothy V. Rasinski, Nancy D. Padak, Brenda Weible Church, Gay Fawcett, Judith Hendershot, Justina M. Henry, Barbara G. Moss, Jacqueline K. Peck, Elizabeth (Betsy) Pryor, Kathleen A. Roskos

From Literature to Literacy: Bridging Learning in the Library and the Primary Grade Classroom—by Joy F. Moss, Marilyn F. Fenster

In the First Few Years: Reflections of a Beginning Teacher—by Tina Humphrey

Journey of Discovery: Building a Classroom Community Through Diagnostic-Reflective Portfolios—by Ann M. Courtney, Theresa L. Abodeeb

Reading to, with, and by Children—by Margaret E. Mooney

Role of Phonics in Reading Instruction: A Position Statement of the International Reading Association—by IRA

Talking Classrooms: Shaping Children's Learning Through Oral Language Instruction—editor: Patricia G. Smith

Teaching Phonics Today: A Primer for Educators—by Dorothy S. Strickland

Tiger Lilies, Toadstools, and Thunderbolts: Engaging K–8 Students with Poetry—by Iris McClellan Tiedt

Worm Painting and 44 More Hands-On Language Arts Activities for the Primary Grades—by E. Jo Ann Belk, Richard A. Thompson

Rocks ....pages 52–53
1. b
2. a
3. d
4. b
5. c

Weather ....pages 54–55
1. b
2. c
3. b
4. c
5. a

The Water Cycle ....pages 56–57
1. a
2. b
3. b
4. d
5. a

Getting Along and Working Together ....pages 59–61
1. c
2. The class wasn't working very well together.
3. b
4. a
5. Answers will vary.

December Celebrations Around the World.....................pages 62–64
1. a
2. b
3. c
4. b
5. a

Shape Guessing Game ...pages 65–67
1. c
2. c
3. b
4. b
5. a

Periods and Exclamation Points ....page 75
Added punctuation is underlined. Some answers may vary.
I went to the zoo on Saturday. It was really fun! We saw many different animals, but the monkeys are my favorite. The monkeys were climbing all around. One almost fell out of a tree! After the zoo, we went to get ice cream. It was a great way to spend the day!

Question Marks.......................page 76
Answers will vary.

Quotation Marks ....page 77
Added punctuation is underlined
Paragraph 1
  "Hi, Tom!" said Jacob.
  "Hi," said Tom.
  "Are you going to play in the game this week?" asked Jacob.
  "If I pass my math test I will. My mom and dad said school comes first," said Tom.
  "Do you need help studying?" asked Jacob.
  "That would be great! I need the help," replied Tom.
  "Well, we need your help in the game, too!" said Jacob. "Let's go study."

Paragraph 2
  "What are you doing?" asked Serita.
  "I'm cleaning my room before Mom gets home," said Deshaun. "Why?"
  "I need your help," replied Serita.
  "With what?" asked Deshaun.
  "I can't find my new markers," said Serita.
  "Well, help me clean my room and then I will help you look," said Deshaun.
  "Okay," said Serita. After a few minutes helping her brother, Serita was surprised. "Hey, I found my markers!" she shouted.
  "Oh yeah, I forgot that I borrowed those from you," said Deshaun. "I must have lost them in my messy room! Sorry!"